# 101 Retail Touchpoints Brainstorming Guide
## *Revised Edition*

*Marketing and advertising quick reference
to reach shoppers in any store and increase sales*

By Lizanne Aponte-Hudo

*This book and the content provided herein are simply for educational purposes and do not take the place of professional advice. Every effort has been made to ensure that the content provided on this book is accurate and helpful for our readers at publishing time. However, this is not an exhaustive treatment of the subjects. No liability is assumed for losses or damages due to the information provided. You are responsible for your own choices, actions, and results. You should consult a professional individual or company to address your business questions and needs.*

**101 Retail Touchpoints Brainstorming Guide** *Revised Edition* © 2020 Lizanne Aponte-Hudo

All rights reserved. No portion of this book may be reproduced in any form without permission from the publisher, except as permitted by U.S. copyright law.

For permissions contact: mistipsdemarketing@gmail.com

ISBN: 9798670106719

*To my son,
my source of strength
and inspiration*

*To my sister N.
for entertaining
and supporting
each and every one
of my crazy
marketing endeavors*

# Table of Contents

Introduction ................................................................ 7

Welcome .................................................................... 9

About this resource ................................................... 11

Guided keyword search terms, explained ............................. 13

Why is it important to have a comprehensive list of touchpoints? .................................................................. 15

How to choose one touchpoint versus another? ..................... 19

The challenge .............................................................. 21

Who are you talking to? ................................................. 25

Using "The List" to create your in-store brand experience ..... 27

"101 Retail Touchpoints" list ......................................... 31

Introduction to "The List" .............................................. 33

Looking at in-store retail touchpoints in today's digital world . 67

Send your feedback ..................................................... 71

About the author .......................................................... 73

Report suspected piracy ............................................... 75

# Introduction

I wrote the first edition to this book in the fall of 2013 for marketers and advertising creatives. My main motivation was to create a physical form of a long list of touchpoints that was building up in my mind since 2005, when I became Creative Director at the new shopper marketing division of the Global Advertising Agency I was working for in my country.

Before 2010, shopper marketing was on its way to becoming a big deal. The principles and best practices were still yet to be written so we were learning by doing.

As we all -retailers, marketers and creatives, trained in traditional advertising- were forced to shift into shopper marketing, internet became our main source of information. However, a good straight-to-the-point thorough list of all possible contact points to connect with consumers in a physical retail environment was hard to find.

It took me three to four months of revisiting my notes, my favorite stores and my internet browsing history to shape the content of this book. For some people it would have been easier to include a selection of pictures with captions and call it a book, but I wanted it to be more than that.

My idea was NOT to create a shopper marketing textbook or album. It was to develop a tool that would help readers easily visualize the whole in-store shopping journey and fast track their research to find current examples and suppliers relevant to their market.

The original version of this book was published as an eBook in January 2014. Since then, it slowly found its way into business settings.

Much to my surprise, it was also adopted by some universities around the world. I became aware of this a little over a year after publishing, when I observed that every three months a new group of fans joined the social media page created for the book. Over the years, it felt good to welcome the usual number of fans that joined our community on each quarter.

One day, I noticed the new group was five times its original size and begin to worry.

> *"Was the content of the book still current?"*
>
> *"Was it relevant to non-US marketing countries?"*
>
> *"Is it useful in the digital era?"*

With these big questions in mind I revisited the content.

This **101 Retail Touchpoints Brainstorming Guide *(Revised Edition)*** includes an expanded section on how to use it to create a unique in-store brand experience, addressing frequently asked question received from readers.

In addition to correcting some typographical errors, I sprinkled new strategies and tips for leveraging some touchpoints functionality.

Also, even when this book is not about Digital Shopper Marketing, there is a new section looking into in-store retail touchpoints in today's digital world.

What you have in your hands is a validated, logical, and current framework with an easy to follow step by step approach.

# Welcome

If you are reading this book, you probably own a store or work in marketing, advertising and retail among many other fields that requires some type of planning

I anticipate you are looking for ways to step up your game and make your life easier when creating a plan to improve your customers' in-store experience and increase sales.

At any point in time, you may be planning to meet one or more of the following objectives:

1. Reach consumers in the right place at the right time with the right message

2. Make it easy for shoppers to find and buy a brand inside the store

3. Make it easy for products, services, organizations or causes to connect and engage shoppers inside any retail environment

4. Use in-store signage to convert shoppers to digital.

5. Make use of unused space to place advertising vehicles, converting wasted space into profits.

Well, consider this your cheat sheet.

I created this guide because I've been in your position many times.

I know how much precious time is invested (or should I say wasted) just making a list of possible contact points; not to mention the endless hours surfing the internet for references and suppliers.

You should know that many of the touchpoints you will read about here are not exclusive for supermarkets and stores.

In many instances they can also be successfully implemented in other retail environments such as quick service restaurants and service shops.

I hope this little treasure saves you time and ignites some easy inspiration for memorable, mind blowing, effective and profitable ideas.

Also, I wish you find it useful to choose the right touchpoints, locate the media and resources to bring your ideas to life and to accomplish your business, brand and/or client objectives.

Wishing you a successful planning,

Lizanne

---

*To enjoy an inside look to insights and examples of the touchpoints discussed in the following pages, ask to join our exclusive Facebook Community for those who purchased this book.*

*You will find the link in the **Send your feedback** section.*

# About this resource

For professionals in marketing and advertising this resource brings together key ingredients to help them brainstorm ideas for in-store communications.

For store owners and managers, it provides a blueprint of almost every possible option that can be leveraged to promote brands, products and offers. This will not only help to improve shoppers' experience; it will also create added value for brands and may represent an additional source of income for the store (by selling the media space to advertisers).

**Here you will find a LIST, yes; but ALSO…**

1. A brief introduction to key aspects I usually take into consideration before initiating any in-store communications brainstorming (i.e. marketing objective and target).

2. Direction in terms of what specific keywords have worked for me to narrow my searches and find visual references and suppliers.

3. Information and insights that I've gathered over the years, that emphasize or expand on relevance and usefulness of certain touchpoints.

However, this book does not aim to provide detailed, academic, or descriptive explanation of in-store communications or strategic marketing planning (other resources are readily available covering these thoroughly).

As a working tool, you can expect this guide will help you accelerate your thinking process by reducing the time usually spent sorting out the multitude of touchpoints available in-store.

# Guided keyword search terms, explained

It is a common practice to use the internet for research and brainstorming. Choosing the right search terms is key to finding the right links and images. However, doing effective research for touchpoints specifically located within the retail environment is not always easy.

The reason for this is that throughout the years many advertising and consumer brands powerhouses have coined words and phrases to describe a phenomenon or trend relevant to their proprietary strategic platforms. For example, *touchpoint* is a term coined a while ago to talk about what is also known as *point-of-contact*, *point-of-engagement* or *interaction point*.

To help you broaden your search but obtain useful relevant results, I am including the usual suspects I use when I want to find up-to-date references for a specific touchpoint or in-store media.

I'm using "*GKS>*" as an abbreviation for **Guided Keyword Search**; so, every time you read *GKS>* you will find a combination of words to write into your search engine to find images and links that illustrate the touchpoint listed above.

---

*Don't forget to click on "Images" to go straight to the pictures.*

---

Yes, some GKS's are more obvious than others; but I will always include hint words when appropriate.

Feel free to add your own terms before or after, to expand or narrow your search as needed (i.e. add the name of your country to find examples or suppliers in your area.)

---

*Remember that adding and removing quote signs (") can also narrow and expand your search, accordingly.*

---

Please note that I refrained from including specific links to save you from the frustrating experience of clicking on a link only to find that the information is no longer available.

Keep in mind that each search engine provides different results according to their particular ranking criteria. If you are not pleased with the results of your initial search, try a different search engine.

# Why is it important to have a comprehensive list of touchpoints?

1) What was usually called "Point-of-Sale" is now also known as "Point-of-Selection"; just because around 70 per cent of purchase decisions are made in-store.

Research done by the In-Store Marketing Institute and the Point-of-Purchase Advertising Institute (POPAI) consistently reported that over two thirds of all purchasing decisions are made at point-of-sale. (Ready to practice? Here's your first GKS.)

**GKS>**
"average shopper's purchase decisions"

Since any brand that wants to be seen or heard will try their best to be loud and bold, having a retail touchpoints guide will make it easier to choose the most relevant contact point or, better yet, could ignite some inspiration to find your unique unleveraged space inside the store.

2) Touchpoints are the building blocks of the customer's brand experience. They are any possible point of contact between the brand and the shopper including but not limited to products, services, transactions, location fixtures or experiences related to your brand.

From TV and digital ads to on-shelf messages, anything that gives the customer an impression of your brand should be considered a touchpoint (even the product itself.)

The more you know about every possible contact point your potential customer may come across with, the more likely you will be able to anticipate their mindset and receptivity at the time you intercept them.

3) In-store communications is the exchange of information between the brand and the customer, which exclusively takes place within the traditional retail environment.

   a. In contrast with traditional media, where consumers tune in a single channel and see one ad after another (i.e. television and print, among other), in-store communications experience is nonlinear. Customers are exposed to hundreds, and sometimes thousands, of brands competing for their attention and their preference, all at the same time.

   b. The in-store environment offers multiple touchpoints. They usually play different roles within a specific strategy (i.e. stopping or interrupting with news, engaging, activating or closing the sale). Location and relevance, in addition to using the appropriate message, are crucial for the successful use of a specific in-store touchpoint.

c. In-store communications can be used to build brands, but marketers have learned that focusing their message on brand equity is not exactly the most appropriate approach if they want to generate sales. What in-store messaging motivates purchase? It depends on the drivers for each specific product category.

Understanding the role and usefulness of touchpoints as communication platforms usually helps in narrowing the most appropriate message to generate the desired action.


4) Choosing the right touchpoints

a. From the marketer's point-of-view it is fair to say that when choosing a touchpoint one must try to make sure it is relevant and helpful to meet one or more of the following: showcase products, engage consumers and/or achieve increased sales.

b. From the shopper's standpoint, the appropriate selection (and use) of touchpoints will be highly appreciated if they help navigate towards products that are hard to find and/or ease the overwhelming experience of having too many options to choose from.

c. From the store owner's perspective, the use of touchpoints should never interfere with the consumer's shopping experience; should never invade products' shelf space and must always observe all types of safety precautions to avoid accidents, injuries and lawsuits, among many other considerations.

# How to choose one touchpoint versus another?

When making the final selection of your touchpoints many variables will come to play (i.e. budget, suppliers' availability, creative, priorities, etc.) To kick start your brainstorming it will be enough to have two things in mind.

1. What is the challenge your brand is/will be facing in-store?
2. Who are you talking to?

(These will be discussed in detail in the following sections.)

Understanding these two aspects will help you determine and weigh in the relevance of each touchpoint.

It should be easier to decide after you find answers to key questions such as: Is it relevant to the brand/product? Is it relevant for the target? Does it help to overcome any specific challenge? How?

# The challenge

To define the challenge(s) simply ask yourself (or the client) why you need to do in-store advertising for that specific brand/product.

The following list can help you narrow the answers and understand how they can translate into possible communication objectives.

## 1) Product launch

**OBJECTIVE A:**
Generate awareness.

**OBJECTIVE B:**
Sometimes, generating trial figures also as an objective.

## 2) Lack of brand recognition

Perhaps, your brand has been on shelves for a long time now, but it is not in top of mind and has no premium position in your potential client's consideration set.

**OBJECTIVE A:**
Generate awareness.

**OBJECTIVE B:**
Position your brand in the top three choices of the consumer's consideration set

## 3) Consumer ignores the product's performance or attributes

**OBJECTIVE A:**
Drive trial

**OBJECTIVE B:**
Educate consumer about product's performance or attributes.

## 4) Limited shelf space

**OBJECTIVE A:**
Increase out-of-shelf in-store inventory.

**OBJECTIVE B:**
Increase product visibility.

## 5) Poor shelf location

**OBJECTIVE A:**
Enhance navigation towards your product/brand.

**OBJECTIVE B:**
Increase on-shelf visibility to make it easy for shoppers to find and buy your product/brand.

## 6) Consumers believe that your product is for a single use

**OBJECTIVE:**
Educate consumers about your product's multiple uses.

## 7) Product's cost is higher than the competition

**OBJECTIVE:**
Educate consumers about the attributes that give value to your product/brand over cheaper options.

## 8) New presentation (i.e. packaging or label)

**OBJECTIVE A:**
Create awareness of new package or label with same quality/price.

**OBJECTIVE B:**
Retain customers of the old presentation.

## 9) Your product is stored in a locked cabinet

**OBJECTIVE A:**
Remind clients to ask for your product at the checkout.

## 10) Other

**OBJECTIVE A:**
Claim /create perception of new leadership/leading brand status.

**OBJECTIVE B:**
Debunk Misconceptions

**OBJECTIVE C:**
Advertise a special promotion

# Who are you talking to?

Aside from your geographic location or local market trends, in-store shoppers can be classified into four major groups, depending on their mental state while shopping.

Knowing who you may be talking to, can help you in your touchpoints' selection.

1. If your potential shopper is always in a hurry you should make sure it is easy for them to find your brand and understand your message. Placing out of aisle displays in the perimeter of staple items (i.e. milk, bread, soda, and the like.) may increase your chances of getting noticed and purchased.

2. If you will be talking to the "inspiration seeker" (the one that plans meals or events while in the store), make sure you provide appetite appeal and easy to follow recipes or guides. Cross selling tactics are useful when you target this type of shopper. When key ingredients of a specific menu are next to each other, it is easier for them to visualize the whole meal and make decision. i.e. eggs and bacon, burgers and fries, spaghetti and meat sauce.

3. Engaging the "stick-to-the-plan" shopper can be more challenging because they usually bring their list and follow a specific path to finalize their purchase.

For these you must be big, bold, entertaining, and convincing to persuade them to do unplanned purchases. Sampling is usually an ideal way to go to intercept this shopper and make them change their game plan.

4. It is very likely that the bargain hunter will find your brand and communication no matter what. However, if you can't provide the best price, you must give them a sound value/performance argument to get your product in their basket.

Always take into consideration if you will be talking to a "solo traveler" or to one or more members of a "shopping brigade".

1. Solo travelers are usually the shopping decision maker and may be choosing for themselves or for a family member that is not present to influence the final decision.

2. On the other hand, shopping brigades are usually composed by the shopper leading the journey and one or more influencers (consumers). Think of married couples or a mom with kids.

# Using "The List" to create your in-store brand experience

"The List" is short for the retail touchpoints inventory included in this book. Even though it provides a catalogue of potential points of contact to include in your plan it is not meant to be used as the single source of information to make your decisions.

## Using research

When research data is available, use it! But please, use it with caution.

Yes, there are many high-priced, well-thought-out, thorough research studies that can ideally help to make your planning easier. However, these types of studies take time.

For this reason, it is not recommended to rely only on the data without taking into consideration any events that might have affected consumers' shopping patterns or transformed the industry landscape.

Think of natural disasters, changes in government, financial crisis' rumors or reality, new FDA and EPA regulations, introduction of new technologies and/or any health crisis that had occurred after the research was published.

When using the retail touchpoints list provided in this book to create your plan, research data can help you validate if a particular touchpoint is a hot contact point worth exploring. Also, it can help justify an investment of a pricier initiative.

When there is no current/relevant research data available, use your better judgment to trace your potential shopper in-store purchase path. If you are not the target, make sure that your "better judgement" is not solely based on your personal experience. Try to look at things from your intended audience point of view and ask the opinion of family members or coworkers with the characteristics of your target audience.

## Store visits

Nothing like an in-person experience navigating the aisles of more than one store to explore, brainstorm and plan.

Using "the list", create a touchpoint map pinpointing ALL the possible shopper's contact, exposure or experiences with your product/brand.

While creating this map, be intentional and exclude nothing. Think about the obvious as well as other key relevant spots where you could disrupt and engage with your potential shopper. i.e. If your client is a razor brand, and their products are kept in a locked cabinet at the service desk, the shaving cream section as well as the grocery checkout are ideal locations to remind your shopper to ask for the product.

## Prioritize your choices

The retail environment provides infinite number of opportunities to engage with shoppers in relevant and creative ways.

Being able to execute a plan with all the ideas you can think of is usually impossible.

To fine-tune your plan, revisit your brief and identify which touchpoints in your map provide to meet each one of your objectives. Highlight those that seem to be the most relevant and influential for your target audience.

For example, if you are launching a new diaper, a demo booth on the baby products aisle is highly recommended to approach and educate your target. Also, leveraging on the expectant mom's parking space is ideal to engage your target at point-of-entry.

Another way to narrow your choices is to look at the options contemplated in your plan through the lens of current relevant research data. Let's look at this with an example.

Imagine you are creating a plan for an eggs brand with the objective to increase sales during Q4 in United States. The obvious touchpoint would be the eggs' aisle. However, in this hypothetical scenario data shows increased sales in the baking products category as well as for products used in eggnog recipes such as milk, cream, vanilla extract, nutmeg spice and brandy. These illustrates other relevant opportunities you could leverage to engage with your prospect.

Other criteria that would definitely impact you final plan include budget, production times, retail marketing cycles, and store policies.

## Design the best brand experience

Choosing the right message for each touchpoint is as important as the touchpoint itself.

Ideally generic messaging should be avoided. Using the same copy content on each contact point may present the risk of boredom or invisibility due to immunization to the message.

As you move forward through the retail touchpoints list presented in the next section, location, reach, relevance and even the physical characteristics shed some light about what the appropriate message could be.

Keep in mind that content, images, giveaways and activities, all play instrumental roles in the in-store brand experience and must fulfill the overall brand promise permeating the whole campaign.

# "101 Retail Touchpoints" List

# Introduction to "The List"

The following list includes specific touchpoints in the last track of the average customer's path-to-purchase. That is, starting at the traffic light or road just before they enter to the store's parking area and ending at the cash register.

You will find any possible point-of-contact I know of for any typical supermarket whether it is an independent store, or an anchor store located outside a shopping mall.

Many of these touchpoints can also be found (or created) in other retail environments such as pharmacies, department stores, mom-and-pop businesses, and convenience shops.

One vital aspect to bear in mind when looking at this list is that at each touchpoint you will be competing for your target audience's attention.

While doing your evaluation, look for other media present or nearby; how many images will your target be exposed to; for how long each person will be exposed to your message; what typical behaviors you can anticipate may interfere with the appreciation of your message (i.e. looking at their cellphones).

Also, ask yourself things like… Does the media or touchpoint feel relevant to your objective? Does it fit in your brand character? Will you be able to measure its effectiveness (if you need to include ROI on your reports)?

One last comment before we dive into the list.

For some touchpoints included, pictures may be hard to find on the web. That does not necessarily mean it has never been done. It could be that if it has been done, no one uploaded photos to the internet. You will still find GKSs that will lead you to images for reference and inspiration, not to actual representation of the ideas.

## A) ROADS LEADING INTO THE STORE'S OR MALL PARKING ENTRANCE

When shoppers are on their way to the store, they are closer to make the mental shift into shopping mode. Some are already thinking about their shopping lists. This makes the perfect opportunity to raise awareness about any brand, product, offer or event the shopper may find or should look for inside the store.

### 1) Billboards
Considered by many a classic to reach people on the go, particularly in big cities and long highways. They are great to impact a great number of prospects but not appropriate for convoluted messages or too much text.

*GKS>*
a) "billboard advertising"

b) "billboard advertising" (insert product category) i.e. Billboard advertising beer

### 2) Bus shelters (Bus stops)
Advertising any products and services at bus stops can provide high profile exposure near point-of-purchase locations.

*GKS>*
"bus shelter advertising"

## 3) Human billboards

Think of a modern version of the sandwich man. A human billboard is someone holding or wearing a promotional sign. Also known as sign walkers, human directional and sign wavers.

*GKS>*

a) "human billboard advertising"

b) "human billboard walking"


## 4) Promoters distributing handouts (i.e. flyers, coupons)

Flyers, also called circulars, or leaflets, are a low-cost form of mass marketing or communication in the form of paper advertisement intended for wide distribution. Not ideal for "green" brands and companies that are self-proclaimed environmental advocates.

*GKS>*

"local flyer distribution"

# B) PARKING AREA

Once the shoppers enter the parking area, they are more likely to make a full mental shift into shopping mode. This means they are more receptive to any brand message and more willing to act upon it.

### 5) Traditional banners
Usually installed on fences, between columns or light poles.

*GKS>*
"outdoor vinyl banner"

### 6) Parking arm gate
Ads are usually displayed in the form of a protective gate arm sleeve. Their appeal consists of demanding the consumer's undivided attention when cars enter and exit the parking area.

*GKS>*
"gate arm advertising"

### 7) Parking booth or security tower
I haven't seen it yet, but wouldn't it be a great idea to wrap a parking booth or security tower with branding? Check the following GSKs for inspiration.

*GKS>*
a) "parking booth"

b) "wrapped booth"

## 8) Light pole banners

Great way to get your message across to the masses. They not also provide to create a festive welcoming environment; they are commonly used to "claim" territory.

*GKS>*
"light pole banner"

## 9) Light pole base cover

Noticeable, cost effective and last longer that light pole banners. They allow to connect with visitors at eye level. The fact that they protect cars from accidents is a bonus.

*GKS>*
"parking light pole base cover logo"

## 10) Parking signs

*GKS>*
"parking promotional pole signs"

## 11) Parking line ads

*GKS>*
"parking stripe advertising"

## 12) Large format outdoor brand exposure (i.e. Inflatables, mobile boards.)

*GKS>*
a) "inflatable advertising"

b) "multimedia LED mobile billboards"


## 13) Pop-Up brand venues
Commonly used to build brand experiences on location such as retailtainment and community programs. They provide to use ambience, emotion, sound and activities to get customers interested in the merchandise or service.

*GKS>*
a) "branded RV"

b) "custom pop up tents"


## 14) Expectant mom parking space
Expecting moms are a vital target for many brands, from baby products to fast-and-easy-to-cook meals, they all pay attention to these women. Since they are becoming a new type of consumer, one of the best ways to engage them is where no one can. Expectant mom parking spaces can be found in many retailers. If they do not exist in your location of interest, talk to the owners and create them!

*GKS>*
a) "expectant mom parking"

b) "stork parking ad"

## 15) Valet parking booth or sign

*GKS>*
"valet parking advertising"


## 16) Other
To find more inspiring examples, with broader searches. i.e. floor graphics on parking lots, ads on parking bumpers, wall graphics and parking ticket executions among many more.

*GKS>*
a) "parking advertising"

b) "parking ambient advertising"

c) "parking ticket advertising"

## C) SHOPPING CARTS AREA (Also known as grocery carts area)

The first thing most people do when they enter a supermarket territory is grab a shopping cart. They keep it in front of them the entire time, and then drop it off near their vehicle. Shopping cart corrals provide high profile exposure for brands that want to approach shoppers early in the last track of the purchase path. On the other hand, advertising in the shopping cart puts the brand's name and message in front of their potential client during the entire shopping trip.

### 17) Shopping cart docking station pole sign

*GKS>*
a) "shopping cart corral sign"

b) "cart corral signage"


### 18) Shopping cart docking station side panels

*GKS>*
a) "shopping cart corral sign"

b) "cart corral signage"

## 19) Shopping cart handle frames

Great opportunity for an "in-your-face" unavoidable advertising touchpoint.

*GKS>*
"shopping cart handle advertising"


## 20) Shopping cart side panels

Shopping cart advertisements installed on one or more sides of the cart, provide brand exposure to shoppers pushing the cart throughout the store. Also, they transform the cart into a moving billboard intercepting shoppers reaching potential clients even if they don't use shopping carts during their visit.

*GKS>*
"grocery cart advertising"


## 21) Shopping cart child seat signs

Another opportunity for an "in-your-face" unavoidable but less intrusive advertising touchpoint.

*GKS>*
"grocery cart advertising"


## 22) Shopping cart front panel sign

*GKS>*
"grocery cart advertising"

## 23) Shopping cart cup holder

This option is highly relevant for brands selling soda, water, juice and any other type of refreshing drinks.

*GKS>*
"grocery cart cup holder"


## 24) Shopping cart handle cover

*GKS>*
a) "shopping cart handle sanitary cover advertising"

b) "shopping cart handle advertising"


## 25) Shopping cart basket bottom liner

*GKS>*
a) "shopping cart bottom advertising"

b) "shopping trolley advertising"


## 26) Shopping cart lower tray (under the basket frame)

*GKS>*
"shopping cart outdoor advert"

[Please note I'm using the word "advert" on purpose. In this instance I recommend including the quote signs to narrow your search.]

## D) GREETING AREA (STORE ENTRANCE)

For those who want to create a full shopper marketing experience, this is another good place to start.

From window decals to floor mats and greeters, use everything big and bold to set the mood and increase your chances to place your brand in consumer's top of mind.

### 27) Entrance door and windows decals

*GKS>*
"grocery store window graphics"

### 28) Door posters/stickers

*GKS>*
a) "retail window poster advertising"

b) "window signs and cling"

### 29) Entrance floor mat

*GKS>*
a) "branded floor mats"

b) "supermarket floor mat advertising insert"

c) "retail floor mat advertising"

## 30) Security checkpoint covers

This option leverages on the largest advertising space available at the entrance of retail stores with 100% visibility to all shoppers. Make sure your supplier has the appropriate patented material that doesn't block the security scanners.

*GKS>*
"store security pedestal advertising"


## 31) Shopper (Weekly Specials Circular)

*GKS>*
"retail weekly circular"


## 32) Shoppers Display Fixture

*GKS>*
"literature stand with poster"


## 33) Coupons

*GKS>*
a) "coupons"

b) "grocery coupons"


## 34) Coupon's display or fixture

*GKS>*
"retail coupon display"

## 35) In-store audio

*GKS>*

"in-store audio sample" [No pics available for these but you will find suppliers with some audio samples.]


## 36) Store greeter

Great spot to introduce your brand or offer to store visitors. You can greet customers via a hologram or a robot at the entrance or simply leverage on the human factor and create vests and name tags for employees.

*GKS>*

"retail greeter campaign"

## E) SHOPPING BASKETS AREA (STORE ENTRANCE)

### 37) Branded shopping baskets

*GKS>*

a) "promotional supermarket handbasket"

b) "promotional supermarket hand basket"


### 38) Shopping basket bottom liners

*GKS>*

a) "advertising supermarket basket"

b) "shopping cart bottom advertising"

c) "grocery cart advertising"


### 39) Shopping basket lateral signs

*GKS>*

a) "shopping basket advertising"

b) "grocery cart advertising"


### 40) Shopping basket stand

*GKS>*

"shopping basket stand"

# F) ON-AISLE

The following are more traditional and expected touchpoints. Still, there is a great opportunity to innovate by incorporating technological elements. i.e. video monitors, interactive digital displays, lenticular signs, QR codes, etc.

## 41) End cap fixture

*GKS>*
"in-store end cap"

## 42) Headers

*GKS>*
a) "in-store communication shelf header signage"

b) "in-store marketing shelf header signage"

## 43) Ceiling Banner

*GKS>*
"ceiling banner"

## 44) Aisle Arches

Great for multiple brand initiatives when the master brand objective is domination.

*GKS>*
"in-store aisle arches"

## 45) Out of Aisle Display/Fixture

Preferred by brands with limited shelf space. Also, a great device to increase visibility. Useful for master brands with multiple products in the same category.

*GKS>*
a) "point-of-purchase display"

b) "pop display"

c) "in-store aisle display"

d) "in-store display"


## 46) Pallets

*GKS>*
"pallet skirt logo"


## 47) Disruptors /Aisle Stoppers

*GKS>*
a) "shelf stopper"

b) "aisle stopper sign"


## 48) Shelf strips

*GKS>*
a) "shelf strips"

b) "shelf video strip"

## 49) Shelf talkers/ Danglers (paper or plastic)

*GKS>*
"shelf talker"


## 50) Shelf talkers/ Danglers (digital)

*GKS>*
"in store advertising on-shelf digital"


## 51) Shelf signage with video display

*GKS>*
a) "supermarket shelf digital signage"

b) "in-store digital sign"


## 52) Shelf signage with coupon dispenser

*GKS>*
"shelf coupon dispenser"


## 53) On-pack coupons

*GKS>*
"on pack coupon"

## 54) Floor graphics

*GKS>*

a) "floor graphics"

b) "3d floor graphics"

c) "supermarket floor graphics"

d) "in-store communication medium floor"


## 55) Floor mats
It is very likely to see these below the shelves of products packaged in glass vases. i.e. baby food. Checkout new models with an ad insert window surrounded with carpet material.

*GKS>*

a) "floor advertising mats"

b) "branded mats"

c) "unusual floor advertising"


## 56) Shelf extender
In addition to creating additional shelf space for you product, some models provide an excellent tool for cross marketing your product in relevant sections.

*GKS>*
"retail shelf extender"


## 57) Sampling kiosks (or demonstration booths)

*GKS>*
"supermarket sampling"


## 58) Mid aisle price scanners

Not available on every store. However, they should be! If your client wants to reach all type of consumers at any cost, they can offer to install fully branded equipment on their key account locations.

*GKS>*
a) "price check scanner"

b) "aisle store price scanner"

## G) FREEZER AISLE

*Revisit the On-Aisle section for ideas that can be used in this area.*

### 59) Door decals

*GKS>*

a) "window signs and cling"

b) "advertising glass door decal"

### 60) Door handles

*GKS>*

a) "door handle campaign"

b) "door handle cover advertising"

### 61) Open freezer signs

*GKS>*

"in-store communication freezer sign"

## H) GROCERY CHECKOUT

This is the ultimate touchpoint inside any retail environment. It is the final opportunity to create purchase intent and drive decision-making towards your product or brand. The following touchpoints are highly relevant for:

- Products relying on impulse purchases (i.e. candy, snaks, soda, and the like.)

- Products stored in locked fixtures such as liquor, razors, infant formula and coffee.

- Promotions and sweepstakes that use coupons or offer special discounts.

### 62) Checkout signs

*GKS>*
"in-store checkout sign"

### 63) Grocery checkout belt

*GKS>*
a) "checkout belt advertising"

b) "checkstand belt cover"

## 64) Employee's name tag (paper, plastic or video)

*GKS>*
a) "employee name badge advertising"

b) "digital name tag"


## 65) Grocery Divider

*GKS>*
"grocery divider ad bar"


## 66) TV Monitors & digital displays

*GKS>*
"grocery digital signage"


## 67) Ceiling banner
Not exactly one of my favorites, I must say. Aside from looking for a specific aisle or department do you really walk around the store looking up to the ceiling? Think about it. Still it is widely used in big department stores and clubs.

*GKS>*
"ceiling banner"


## 67) Purchase receipt ads & coupons

*GKS>*
"grocery receipt advertising"

## 68) Bags

In countries that have said no to plastic grocery store bags, paper bags are still a good option.

***GKS>***
a) "branded shopping plastic bag"

b) "branded grocery bags"

c) "branded eco-friendly plastic bags"

## I) MEAT DEPARMENT

Meat centers are ideal touchpoints for cross marketing campaigns of brands that sell meat sauce, spices, side dishes and wines.

---

*Revisit the On-Aisle section for ideas that can be used in this area.*

---

### 69) Meat center

*GKS>*
a) "meat department advertising"


### 70) Menu board

*GKS>*
"branded menu board"


### 71) Take-a-number tabs dispenser

*GKS>*
"take a number sign"


### 72) Recipe dispenser

*GKS>*
a) "shelf dispenser"

b) "coupon display"

## J) RESTROOMS

### 73) Cubicle doors

*GKS>*
"cubicle door wrap advertising"


### 74) Mirrors

*GKS>*
"restroom mirror advertising"


### 75) Soap Dispenser Ads

*GKS>*
"soap dispenser guerrilla"


### 76) Beauty styling vending machines (i.e. blow dryer and flat iron for public restrooms).

*GKS>*
"hair iron vending machine"


### 77) Toilet tissue dispenser

*GKS>*
"toilet ambient advertising tissue"

## 78) Towel tissue dispenser

*GKS>*
"bathroom towel dispenser advertising"

## 79) Hand dryer

*GKS>*
a) "hand dryer advertising"

b) "hand dryer marketing"

## 80) Toilet rug shape ads

*GKS>*
a) "toilet rug advertising"

b) "toilet floor graphics"

"

## 81) Wet Floor Caution Sign

*GKS>*
"wet floor creative ambient"

## 82) Baby Changing Station

*GKS>*
a) "baby changing station guerrilla"

b) "baby changing station advertising"

## 83) Urinals

*GKS>*
"urinal advertising"

# K) DELI

## 84) Table tents

*GKS>*

"table tent advertising"

## 85) Table tops

*GKS>*

"tabletop advertising"

## 86) Salt & pepper shakers

*GKS>*

"salt pepper shaker advertising"

## 87) Napkins

*GKS>*

"napkin advertising"

## 88) Napkin dispenser

*GKS>*

"napkin dispenser advertising"

## 89) Tray liners

*GKS>*
"tray liner advertising"


## 90) Menu board

*GKS>*
"menu board advertising"

## L) CLIENT SERVICE AREA

### 91) Information desk, counter or podium

*GKS>*
a) "supermarket customer service desk"

b) "customer service sign"


### 92) Counter card and/or counter card display

*GKS>*
"counter card display"


### 93) Crowd control barriers

*GKS>*
"crowd control signage advertising"


### 94) Newspaper Stands

*GKS>*
a) "newspaper stand"

b) "newspaper stand fixture"


### 95) Leaflets and leaflets dispensers

*GKS>*
"leaflet dispenser"

# M) OTHER

### 96) Elevators

*GKS>*
"elevator advertising"

### 97) Escalators

*GKS>*
"escalator advertising"

### 98) Trashcans

*GKS>*
a) "trash can advertising"

b) "garbage bin advertising"

### 99) Ceiling displays

*GKS>*
a) "ceiling advertising"

b) "ceiling display"

## 100) Above eye level (in columns, above aisles, endcaps and other fixtures)

*GKS>*
"grocery digital signage"

*GKS>*
a) "branded freezer"

b) "branded ice freezer"

c) "outdoor ice cooler"

d) "ice freezer"


## 101) SMS or text message marketing platform
The way to offer personalized promotional discounts at POS. The increasing use of smartphones has consumer packaged goods companies investing in ads on the go. Tapping into mobile marketing offers supermarket brands the opportunity to deliver targeted promotions.

*GKS>*
a) "retail text message marketing"

b) "text marketing"

# Looking at in-store retail touchpoints in today's digital world

Smartphones are everywhere and the number of consumers on their phone while shopping is increasing by the minute.

They could be distracted in a non-shopping related conversation which makes in-store communication more necessary than ever. The fact that their attention span may be shortened and even diluted, demands disruptive clever ideas with straight to the point relevant messages.

On the other side of the spectrum, shoppers on the phone while shopping could be looking at product reviews and specs, searching for comparable brands and, hunting deals and discounts, including digital coupons.

*This new reality of shoppers avidly digesting digital content while shopping, forces retailers and brands to think of phones (hence, the entire internet) as an omnipresent retail touchpoint in consumers in-store purchase path.*

Since the physical & digital retail worlds have collided, point-of-purchase marketing is no longer restricted to in-store communication. Consequently, your plan to leverage on in-store shoppers' experience must span both worlds.

Whether you are a business owner creating a plan for your store or a marketing professional working on an in-store shopper marketing recommendation for a client, the following tips may help you conquer your prospect amid the impact of digital distractions or interference.

1. Have a digital presence and be consistent in your message in-store and online. Make sure your online presence provides a "place" for shoppers to find relevant information and ask questions.

2. Monitor the conversations about your brand on social media and other forums and react when necessary in a timely, friendly, and professional manner.

3. Do not rely solely on digital platforms for shoppers to find information that could easily be shared in-store. Your objective must be to improve and enrich the shoppers in-store experience. Do not create an obstacle course for them to find information necessary to make their decisions.

You may feel that incorporating digital assets in your in-store communication to connect with shoppers and influence their behavior may have become a necessary evil.

Well, be happy to know that using digital in store is not always necessary or relevant.

When in doubt I encourage you to revisit the section titled "Who you are talking to". Hurry shoppers and those leading a shopping brigade might not have time to look at their phones while shopping.

Also, your digital presence as well as the use of online platforms must be intentional and stay current. If for any reason you cannot keep your website up to date, add true value and manage your digital assets daily, you may be hurting your brand or your relationship with your customers, and wasting money.

# Send your feedback

I hope this guide was useful to you, and I thank you for taking the time to read it.

Is there any touchpoint you think should have been included in this list? Let me know!

Feel free to send your comments, constructive criticism, and suggestions. Your feedback will help me improve this guide for future owners.

---

*Enjoy an inside look of insights and examples of touchpoints shared in this book, by joining our exclusive community of legit book owners at www.facebook.com/groups/rtbg2vip.*

---

Don't forget to tell your friends and colleagues about this guide.

Lizanne Aponte-Hudo
*mistipsdemarketing@gmail.com*

# About the author

In case you wonder what qualifies me to write this guide, I can say that I'm a Marketing Communications professional with strong passion for consumer behavior and market trends that impact the retail environment.

My experience includes a unique combination of shopper marketing, strategic planning and the development of copy and creative for advertising and events to help build insight-based programs to drive company growth and add value to clients, people and processes.

Among many things, I've created campaigns and programs for global brands such as Procter and Gamble, McDonalds and Heineken; at leading agencies including Leo Burnet and Grey Worldwide, for the specific implementation in Puerto Rico and the Caribbean markets.

After two decades working for Corporate America, I continue helping clients as a Strategic Creative Marketing Consultant for brands like Clorox, Unilever among other in the Puerto Rico market.

Visit **www.facebook.com/mistipsdemarketing** to explore more marketing tips and my recent years' journey through eCommerce and Print-On-Demand.

# Report suspected piracy

Dear reader,

The easy availability of pirated works online affects the entire book publishing community, including YOU, publishers, booksellers and more importantly the authors.

The effects of piracy can range from lost sales to the decline in the perception of the value of a book.

More importantly, it forces authors that share their knowledge through publishing for a living, to find other secure ways to protect their income that are usually more expensive and less accessible for readers like you.

Please help us combat digital piracy, protect our content, and the <u>added benefits our readers receive through social media</u>. Join us in helping to protect this work by participating in our anti-piracy efforts.

Thanks for sending us a heads-up about any possible illegal copy you may have found of this book, with as much details as possible, to mistipsdemarketing@gmail.com.

Every notification will be handled in strict confidence and will be highly appreciated.

Sincerely,

Lizanne

amcontent.com/pod-product-compliance
Source LLC
urg PA
147240526
300024BA/1805